W9-APD-366

First Facts™

Everyday Character Education

Cooperation

by Janet Riehecky

Consultant:
Madonna Murphy, PhD, Professor of Education
University of St. Francis, Joliet, Illinois
Author, *Character Education in America's Blue Ribbon Schools*

Capstone
press

Mankato, Minnesota

First Facts is published by Capstone Press,
151 Good Counsel Drive, P.O. Box 669, Mankato, Minnesota 56002.
www.capstonepress.com

Copyright © 2005 by Capstone Press. All rights reserved.
No part of this publication may be reproduced in whole or in part, or stored in a retrieval system, or transmitted in any form or by any means, electronic, mechanical, photocopying, recording, or otherwise, without written permission of the publisher.
For information regarding permission, write to Capstone Press,
151 Good Counsel Drive, P.O. Box 669, Dept. R, Mankato, Minnesota 56002.
Printed in the United States of America

Library of Congress Cataloging-in-Publication Data
Riehecky, Janet, 1953–
    Cooperation / by Janet Riehecky.
    p. cm.—(First facts. Everyday character education)
    Includes bibliographical references and index.
    ISBN 0-7368-3678-0 (hardcover)
    ISBN 0-7368-5146-1 (paperback)
    1. Cooperativeness—Juvenile literature. I. Title. II. Series: First facts. Everyday character education.
BJ1533.C74R54 2005
179'.9—dc22   2004018352

Summary: Introduces cooperation through examples of everyday situations where this character trait can be used.

Editorial Credits
Amanda Doering, editor; Molly Nei, set designer; Kia Adams, book designer; Wanda Winch, photo researcher

Photo Credits
Capstone Press/Gary Sundermeyer, 13 (top right, bottom right); Jim Foell, 13 (top left, bottom left)
Excerpt from–*Lewis and Clark at Three Forks*, E.S. Paxson, Oil on Canvas, 1912, Courtesy of the Montana Historical Society, Don Beatty, photographer 10/1999, 16
Gem Photo Studio/Dan Delaney, cover, 1, 5, 6–7, 8, 9, 10–11, 19
Minden Pictures/Michael & Patricia Fogden, 20
Ryan's Well Foundation/Susan Hreljac, 15

1 2 3 4 5 6 10 09 08 07 06 05

Table of Contents

Cooperation

Nick and Sarah want to play with building blocks. They decide to cooperate. Nick and Sarah decide what to build. They make a plan. They work together to build a rocket.

Fact!
Cooperation is working together to get something done. Cooperation is also following rules and laws so things run smoothly.

At Your School

You can use cooperation at school. Work with other students on group projects. Decide who is best for each part of the project. A good writer can write the report. Whoever draws well can do the artwork. By cooperating, you get more done in less time.

With Your Friends

Good friends cooperate. When playing a game, play by the rules. Cooperation makes sure the game is fair.

Building a sandcastle takes
cooperation. Listen to your friends'
ideas. Be willing to change your plans
if someone has a better idea.

At Home

At home, cooperation keeps everything running smoothly. Pass food around the table until everyone gets some.

Families that cooperate get more done. Work together on **chores**. Your family will have more time for fun activities.

In Your Community

People work together to make their
communities safer, more pleasant places
to live. Police officers keep our streets
safe. Doctors and nurses help people who
are sick or hurt. Teachers help students
learn. Construction workers build new
homes and businesses.

Ryan Hreljac

In first grade, Ryan Hreljac learned that some Africans didn't have clean water. Ryan did extra chores to earn money for WaterCan. This **organization** builds **wells** in poor countries.

Fun Fact!

Ryan now has his own organization. It's called Ryan's Well Foundation. His group has helped build wells in eight countries.

Ryan didn't have enough money to pay for a well by himself. He asked other people to give money. With their cooperation, Ryan raised enough money to build a well in Africa.

Lewis and Clark

In 1803, Meriwether Lewis and William Clark were sent to gather information about the western United States. Lewis and Clark cooperated to make the trip successful. Clark kept a journal of what they saw. He made maps of the land. Lewis spoke to American Indians they met. He collected plants and animals to bring back.

What Would You Do?

Nick and Laura want to play softball. They both want to pitch. Laura says she will quit if she doesn't get to pitch. How should Nick cooperate with Laura so they both get to pitch?

Fun Fact!

In 1998, 15 countries began building a space station. One country couldn't have done it alone. By cooperating, all 15 countries can do experiments from space.

Amazing but True!

Even animals cooperate in communities. In an anthill, each ant has a job. Some ants look for food. Other ants repair the hill. A queen lays eggs. Other ants take care of the eggs. If one ant dies, another ant takes over its job.

Hands On: Three-Legged Race

Playing games takes cooperation. Cooperate with your partner to win this race.

What You Need

5 pieces of thin rope
4 people

What You Do

1. Put down one piece of rope as the finish line. Walk 25 steps away from the finish line. The race will start here.
2. Choose partners.
3. Put your partner on your left side. Both of you should face the finish line. With the rope, tie your left ankle to your partner's right ankle. Tie your left thigh to your partner's right thigh. The other team should do the same.
4. On the count of three, both teams walk toward the finish line. The team who gets to the finish line first wins the race.

Glossary

chore (CHOR)—a job that has to be done regularly; washing dishes and taking out the garbage are chores.

community (kuh-MYOO-nuh-tee)—a group of people who live in the same area

organization (or-guh-nuh-ZAY-shuhn)—people joined together for a certain purpose; WaterCan and Ryan's Well Foundation are organizations that build wells for people in poor countries.

well (WEL)—a deep hole from which you can get water

Read More

Nettleton, Pamela Hill. *Pitch In!: Kids Talk about Cooperation.* Kids Talk. Minneapolis: Picture Window Books, 2004.

Scheunemann, Pam. *Working Together.* Keeping the Peace. Edina, Minn.: Abdo, 2004.

Internet Sites

FactHound offers a safe, fun way to find Internet sites related to this book. All of the sites on FactHound have been researched by our staff.

Here's how:

1. Visit *www.facthound.com*
2. Type in this special code **0736836780** for age-appropriate sites. Or enter a search word related to this book for a more general search.
3. Click on the **Fetch It** button.

FactHound will fetch the best sites for you!

Index